FINDING JOY IN THE JOURNEY

FINDING JOY IN THE JOURNEY

DIAN SUSTEK

Finding Joy in the Journey

Copyright © 2016 by Dian Sustek Published by Grace Theology Press.

Unless otherwise noted, all scripture taken from the New King James Version®. Copyright © 1982 by Thomas Nelson. Used by permission. All rights reserved. ISBNs below.

ISBN 10: 0-9965614-6-3
ISBN 13: 978-0-9965614-6-4
eISBN 10: 0-9965614-7-1
eISBN 13: 978-0-9965614-7-1

Special Sales: Most Grace Theology Press titles are available in special quantity discounts. Custom imprinting or excerpting can also be done to fit special needs. Contact Grace Theology Press at info@gracetheology.org.

Printed in the United States of America

This book is dedicated to my son and daughter-in-love, Scott and Erin Sustek, and to my daughter and son-in-love, Courtney and Greg Fleischman, and to my seven grands! Without your love and support, I would not have been able to walk through such a journey. We cried together, laughed together, loved together and prayed together. I thank my sweet Jesus for each and every one of you.

CONTENTS

FOREWORD

Several months before my husband John died, we went to lunch with friends who had walked this path with us from the beginning. I remember it was Mother's Day and we were at Landry's. Because of something wonderful that God had done for John, his good friend and Pastor, Dave Anderson told him he should write a book about all that he had gone through concerning the joy that God had given him because he had never heard of anything like this ever happening to anyone else. Betty, Dave's wife, and I agreed and we encouraged John to do just that! When we got home, I could tell John was beginning to get excited about the new project. At this point, John would get so obsessed about things he was thinking about, he couldn't focus on anything else but what was going through his mind. That very night he stayed up all night writing his book on his phone. Had he lived, this would have been the way his book began.

"I was born on October 20, 1944, in a bank in Del Rio, Texas. I was a deposit, not a withdrawal..." John started from the beginning, obsessing over every detail that he could remember about his childhood, his years in grade school and on through his years at Rice up until he and I met and married. He never had the time to get to the part that Dave had wanted him to write. And while our family listened as he tried to get things straight in his mind up until a matter of a week or so before he died, I knew I had to tell the account of what was truly the most miraculous thing I had ever witnessed. This is his story, but it's also very much mine.

Have you ever asked the question: "God, how can I know you more intimately?" When I asked that question, I was talking about knowing Him deeply, realizing He was all I needed and feeling Him with me all the time—like I knew John. I suppose I was really asking: "How can I actually experience You, Lord?" His answer was not what I had expected—cancer. Not my own, that would have been preferable. His answer was cancer in the one I loved most. But let me add—if you do not get to know the word of God before a trial or tragedy comes, it will be very difficult to see the hand of God in the midst of the trial. Many voices vie for your attention daily and it's very difficult to hear the voice of God when you haven't studied or been in an abiding relationship with Him in prayer and His Word. Fellowshipping with Him allows you to recognize His ways and detect the lies that the enemy and the world throw at you.

This book is our story. Honestly, it's my story after the love of my life graduated to his forever home! It's about the most horrible yet God-ordained thing that has ever happened to me. God has impressed on me that I am to share it. I never would have chosen this path, and I can honestly tell you that until two years after losing the one I loved intimately for 46 years, I thought I would never be whole again. BUT GOD…every good story is a gospel story! Remember, this isn't about me…it's about God and the story He has written on my heart. He is writing a story on yours, too—and as you read mine, I hope that you will begin thinking of where you are in yours. You won't know He is writing your story unless you make a conscious effort to watch what God is doing. My challenge for you as you read this is that you will make a decision during each event in your life—to see God's hand in your circumstances.

As I was praying about writing my account of walking with my sweet John through his battle with cancer, I remembered a song by Francesca Battisteli that John and I heard many times driving to and from MDACC (M.D. Anderson Cancer Center). WRITE YOUR STORY ON MY HEART. I wasn't sure then, but as time went on and I prayed, I began to realize that God was indeed writing HIS STORY on MY HEART and on the heart of my husband. And now, I believe He has asked me to share it with you.

With that said, here it is. It's been a lot more difficult to write than I had thought because it has caused me to recall many times when John and I laughed and cried together. It has made me come to grips with the fact that my life will never be the same again, but that I wouldn't want it to because God in His grace has grown me into a gentler, kinder and more compassionate woman, so that I can minister to others who need to know that there is comfort and surprisingly, joy after the death of the better part of you.

YAY GOD!

This is my doing ... 1 Kings 12:24

I'm not going all the way back to when we got married because that isn't what this book is about—besides that's a whole other story! But when John and I were getting married, just as with anyone when they're standing at the altar looking into one another's eyes, I never thought about the time a funeral would come. I thought of our hopes and dreams and a wonderful life together, but my mind somehow never (thankfully) went to the place of what would happen if one of us was taken to heaven and the other was left to figure out life apart from that person. What a blessing that our minds were on the moment and perhaps a little bit on the immediate future of the honeymoon!

When John turned 60, I asked him to have a complete physical because he hadn't had one since he retired five years before. He had always been healthy—very seldom did he even get a virus or a cold. He had played basketball and ran track all through junior high and high school, and in college he played softball. He fished and played golf on any day that ended in "Y" and he loved being outdoors. Until he retired, he also had regular physicals. He agreed that it was time for a physical, so in January of 2005 he had one which included a PSA test. That test came back with a high number, so he went to a urologist and had a biopsy. We assumed there would be no problem and kind of forgot about it. On February 1, 2005, we were sitting in the sunroom each doing a devotional, and this is what I read from L. B. Cowman's

STREAMS IN THE DESERT [1]
"February 1: This is my doing. (1 Kings 12:24)"
The disappointments of life are simply the hidden appointments of love. C. A. Fox

My child, I have a message for you today. Let me whisper it in your ear so any storm clouds that may arise will shine with glory, and the rough places you may have to walk will be made smooth. It is only four words, but let them sink into your inner being, and use them as a pillow to rest your weary head. "This is my doing."

Have you ever realized that whatever concerns you concerns Me too? "For whoever touches you touches the apple of [my] eye" (Zech. 2:8). "You are precious and honored in my sight" (Isa. 43:4). Therefore it is My special delight to teach you.

I want you to learn when temptations attack you, and the enemy comes in "like a pent-up flood" (Isa. 59:19), that "this is my doing" and that your weakness needs My strength, and your safety lies in letting Me fight for you.

Are you in difficult circumstances, surrounded by people who do not understand you, never ask your opinion, and always push you aside? This is my doing—I am the God of circumstances. You did not come to this place by accident, you are exactly where I meant for you to be."

"Are you experiencing a time of sorrow? "This is my doing."
I am "a man of sorrows, and familiar with suffering" (Isa. 53:3).

---

[1] Excerpt From: L. B. E. Cowman & Jim Reimann. "Streams in the Desert." iBooks. https://itun.es/us/de_gx.l

I have allowed your earthly comforters to fail you, so that by turning to Me you may receive "eternal encouragement and good hope" (2 Thess. 2:16).

Have you longed to do some great work for Me but instead have been set aside on a bed of sickness and pain? "This is my doing." You were so busy I could not get your attention, and I wanted to teach you some of My deepest truths. "They also serve who only stand and wait." In fact, some of My greatest workers are those physically unable to serve, but who have learned to wield the powerful weapon of prayer.

Today I place a cup of holy oil in your hands. Use it freely, My child. Anoint with it every new circumstance, every word that hurts you, every interruption that makes you impatient, and every weakness you have. The pain will leave as you learn to see Me in all things. Laura A. Barter Snow

"This is from Me," the Savior said,
As bending low He kissed my brow
"For One who loves you thus has led.
Just rest in Me, be patient now,
Your Father knows you have need of this,
Though, why perhaps you cannot see—
Grieve not for things you've seemed to miss.
The thing I send is best for thee."
Then, looking through my tears, I plead,
"Dear Lord, forgive, I did not know,
It will not be hard since You do tread,
Each path before me here below."
And for my good this thing must be,
His grace sufficient for each test.
So still I'll sing, "Whatever be
God's way for me is always best."

I remember looking at John with my mouth open and him saying, "Wow! That was powerful!" We both talked for a while about how many people go through trials all the time and with each one of them, we had noticed that one of two things happens. Either they become angry with God and are frantically trying to get good counsel from man, or they are driven closer to God and seek His wisdom and HE leads them to good counsel. We agreed that we would HOPE and pray that if we were ever in a difficult circumstance we would run to Jesus and seek His will for our walk.

We had walked through several extremely difficult circumstances throughout our marriage. I would mention them but suffice it to say that they were tests to strengthen our faith and grow us up in Jesus. With each challenge, we cried and prayed and wondered what good could possibly come out of what seemed so heartbreaking. But as we grew closer to Jesus, both of us began to understand and take to heart the sovereignty of God and that in His sovereignty, nothing touches us that has not been allowed by God. Many times in the late '80s and through the '90s, we claimed *Romans 8:28—"for we know that ALL THINGS work together for good to those who love God, to those who are called according to HIS PURPOSES!"* And the Bible goes on to say what HIS purpose is: "for whom He foreknew, He also predestined *to be conformed to the image of His Son* that He might be the firstborn among many brethren." If you had known me then, you would have known that was NOT my thought! MY THOUGHT WOULD HAVE BEEN VERY DIFFERENT but this was obviously the work of the Holy Spirit speaking to my heart, for it seemed that each trial we walked through at those times seemed harder than the one before. BUT GOD…God gave me Romans 8:28 to cling to, and cling to it I did. God is faithful—He never changes—and I was determined to keep my eyes on Him. Did you get that? GOD NEVER CHANGES —HE IS THE SAME YESTERDAY, TODAY AND FOREVER! (Hebrews 13:8—Jesus Christ is the same yesterday, today and forever.)

Circumstances change, times change, people change—but God never does. And just in case you've never finished reading the rest of Romans 8, I'll put it in right now because these verses brought me much comfort at a time when I was extremely depressed and concerned about one of our grown children. Romans 8:29–39—"For whom He foreknew He also predestined to be conformed to the image of His Son, that He might be the firstborn among many brethren. Moreover whom He predestined, these He also called; whom He called, these He justified; and whom He justified, these He also glorified. What then shall we say to these things? *If God is for us, who can be against us?* He who did not spare His own Son, but delivered Him up for us all, how shall he not with Him also freely give us all things? Who shall bring a charge against God's elect? It is God who justifies. Who is he who condemns? It is Christ who died and furthermore is also risen who is even at the right hand of God, who also makes intercession for us. Who shall separate us from the love of Christ? Shall tribulation or distress, or persecution, or famine, or nakedness, or peril or sword? As it is written: "For Your sake we are killed all day long—we are accounted as sheep for the slaughter." Yet in all these things we are more than conquerors through Him who loved us. FOR I AM PERSUADED THAT NEITHER DEATH NOR LIFE, NOR ANGELS NOR DEMONS NOR PRINCIPALITIES NOR POWERS NOR THINGS PRESENT NOR THINGS TO COME, NOR HEIGHT NOR DEPTH, NOR ANY OTHER CREATED THING, shall be able to separate us from the love of God which is in Christ Jesus our Lord!"

I have to say that I thank God that He spoke those words to Paul and penned them because I claimed them at a time when I needed to hear truth from the Holy Spirit—a time when I was worried sick over both of our children. I was beginning to understand during that time what it meant to know God intimately. It began to happen further back than even then, but that's when I really realized that having a deep personal relationship would be the most wonderful thing that could ever happen to me or anyone else.

Around 3 p.m. on February 1, 2005, the same day I read the devotional to John from *Streams in the Desert*, we got a call from John's doctor that he not only had prostate cancer but the biopsy showed cancer in all four quadrants of the prostate. To make a long story short, the cancer had already escaped the prostate and had spread.

I wish I could say that we immediately said, "YAY GOD! A CHANCE TO BRING YOU GLORY! THANK YOU FOR GIVING US THAT DEVOTIONAL THIS MORNING! NOW WE GET TO KNOW THAT THIS IS FROM YOU!" But the truth is, I ran to the bathroom and threw up for about half an hour, then the other end turned against me while all this time John was on the phone with his doctor. Once I finally settled down, which took more time than you can imagine, I washed my face and hands, walked into his office, we stood for a long time holding one another and then I said, "OK, now what do we do?" John looked me in the eye and said, "According to our devotional this morning, *this is from God,* so we better ask HIM!"

And that's exactly what we did. We got on our knees and consulted with the One who created us, redeemed us, saved us, was sanctifying us and would one day take us to live with Him forever. He gave each of us a verse that we were to walk in for however long this journey would take. Mine was the first verse I had ever memorized. *1 Thes 5:16-18—"Rejoice always, pray without ceasing, in everything give thanks; for (because) this is the will of God in Christ Jesus for you."* John's verse was James 1:2-4. *"My brethren, count it all joy when you fall into various trials, knowing that the testing of your faith produces patience. But let patience have its perfect work SO THAT you may be perfect and complete, lacking nothing."*

To no surprise, both verses contained the word JOY! I say no surprise because joy had been a theme throughout our marriage. God gave me that scripture when we first moved to Miami—me kicking and screaming and crying because I had *never lived outside the great state of Texas!* Even our two children—one 14 and the other 10— were not happy about this move. After all, we had never lived outside Texas; all of our friends and family were there! But as soon as they saw the beach, they were delighted and ready to begin a new life in Florida. John was an avid fisherman, and of course, HE LOVED IT! Me, not so much. But God had His reasons for moving us out of our comfort zones. Especially me. A man at John's office told him about a Bible teaching church not far from where we lived and that very first Sunday, we showed up. It was June and hotter and more humid than Houston. Scott and Courtney made friends easily and I met lots of women and joined the women's Bible study. Then it happened—we were standing in church one Sunday singing HE LIVES and suddenly it connected—my feeble brain made the connection that HE. LIVES. Now as a child, I had believed that Jesus had died for my sins and that I was going to heaven. And I know that because I believe once saved, always saved—faith alone in Christ alone—but all of a sudden, those words just penetrated my heart! HE LIVES! HE DIDN'T JUST DIE ON THAT CROSS, HE ROSE AND IS ALIVE! I wanted to scream Y'ALL, HE'S ALIVE! ALL OF THIS IS TRUTH! EVERYTHING IS REAL! Goodness, I was laughing and crying and John and the kids thought I was having some sort of breakdown! But it was soon after that they noticed a change in me—I put into practice a verse I had memorized. Whenever I got frustrated and wanted to pitch a hissy fit, I remembered that I was to be joyful, pray and give thanks. I began singing praise songs and praying not just to ask God for things but to thank Him for what He had already given me—how He had protected me and my family. I even began to THANK HIM for us living in Miami, something I had thought would be impossible to ever do! I had a new life—John claimed he had a new wife. Amazing what God's Word can do if you put it into practice, isn't it? It would be many years before I would be given that verse again. As it turns out, it became my life verse. 1 Thess. 5:16-18—"Rejoice always, pray without ceasing, in everything give thanks; for (because) this is the will of God in Christ Jesus for you."

Well, after a trip to the urologist a few days after we got the news, we spoke to a friend at our church who had just finished radiation at the M.D. Anderson satellite in The Woodlands. He gave us the name of his oncologist there, and we called to make an appointment. One reason we wanted this particular oncologist was because she was a strong Christian, and we knew we would need much prayer support and having a praying doctor meant to us that she would seek God's wisdom as she treated her patients. We were told to bring John's records from the urologist when we came to our appointment. I say "our" because when you or someone you love is diagnosed with cancer, the whole family has cancer. It becomes a family affair. Everyone in the family is affected by cancer. *Cancer, like sin, hurts everyone.*

When we got to MDACC, John signed in and we sat down in the waiting room. We were talking and laughing about things that had happened a few days before, and a woman was sitting across the room from us and asked if we were waiting for someone in the back. We told her no; we were waiting to see our radiation oncologist, Dr. Pam. She asked which of us had cancer, and John said he did and that this was our first appointment. She said, "Then what do you have to laugh or smile about?" John said, "We have joy in that we know that cancer, while it will be a trial, is not all there is! God has given us joy in the journey." She just shook her head as they called her name. We prayed for her as she went back. And that began our mission—to share the love of Christ with everyone we met and let them know that He is our hope of glory, and He can be their's too. Not five minutes went by before a chaplain walked in and heard us talking about how excited we were that God would use us as we walked this path. He came over and said, "Excuse me, folks, I couldn't help but overhear your conversation about being used by God as you experience cancer. I'm a chaplain here, and I'm wondering how you can both be so cheerful?" A long conversation followed about how the Holy Spirit gave each of us a verse we were to walk in during this journey. We gave him the verses, and he smiled. Then he said, "May I place a cross of ashes on your foreheads as today is Ash Wednesday and I know that as Christians you both understand what Christ did on that cross?" We said yes, and then we all prayed together. That day was the first of many wonderful encounters with people who were either with those who had cancer or had cancer themselves. And that day we decided that whatever happened, we would walk through those doors with joy and the expectation of bringing glory to God!

When they called John's name, we went in with hope and joy. When Dr. Pam walked in and introduced herself to us, we knew we had made the right decision. She radiated the love of God through her face and her body language. And after the appointment, she took us into a small conference room, and she prayed with and for us. It was as though we had known her forever. Over the following seven years or so, we became friends not only with her, but with her sweet husband and many of her staff. Had God not placed us with her, our journey through cancer would have been so much more difficult than it was.

Can you remember a time when you went through a trial and how you responded to that circumstance? Each of us has a choice of how we will respond to bad news—will we respond with faith or react in fear? I believe that whichever we do we must determine in our hearts BEFORE the time comes and then make it a habit to choose faith over fear. Once John and I did that, we told our faces to match our choice!

LOOK AT THE WORDS 'REJOICE AND JOY' IN THE SCRIPTURES

1 Thess. 5:16-18—"Rejoice always, pray without ceasing, in everything give thanks; for (because) this is the will of God in Christ Jesus for you."

James 1:2-4—"My brethren, count it all joy when you fall into various trials, knowing that the testing of your faith produces patience. But let patience have its perfect work SO THAT you may be perfect and complete, lacking nothing.

OBSERVE HOW THEY ARE USED IN THE PASSAGE and write out your thoughts.

VERIFY USING A DICTIONARY and write out the meaning of both rejoice and joy.

LOOK FOR EXAMPLES OF THOSE IN THE BIBLE WHO WALKED THROUGH HARD THINGS...for example—look at the life of David. Then jot down a few of the ways he either reacted in fear or responded in faith to his circumstances. What did you notice? Was he consistent, or was each experience different?

Father, I know that you are sovereign and that everything that comes to me is allowed by You for a reason. Please help me to count it all joy when I fall into various trials knowing that you have a plan even in the difficult times—and that plan is ultimately for my good and Your glory.

COUNT IT ALL JOY

James 1:2 ... My brethren, count it all joy
WHEN you fall into various trials...

J ohn took a total of 42 radiation treatments and as a treat for being finished, we flew to Hawaii with a group of friends for a golfing trip. These were people we had been friends with for years, and they had all been praying for his treatments to be a success. It was a great time with great friends and such a relief not to be going back and forth everyday for treatment! He felt so good for the next couple of months that we forgot about the cancer, thinking he was probably cured. Unfortunately his next blood workup showed that the radiation had been ruled unsuccessful. Our next step was chemotherapy. So we were going to have the opportunity to go to the big campus of M.D. Anderson downtown to spread more joy. (Well, that exact thought was not my first one!)

I'll never forget when James 1:2–4 was claimed for the first time by my husband. It was after the first day of testing, poking and prodding at MDACC in the medical center. Our appointment downtown was at 7 a.m. for blood work and then at 9 a.m. to meet his oncologist, Dr. John, a young man younger than our son, whom we liked very much. He mentioned how happy we seemed, and John told him the story of what God had done by giving us joy in this journey. He said we were the first to ever tell him that! The next order of business was a second Lupron shot—bless his heart—he hated what Lupron did to him. The first one he took was the first day of treatment in The Woodlands—Lupron kills all testosterone in the body. Testosterone causes prostate cancer to grow so they attack that first! A quick side-note, that evil Lupron was a curse to him, but a blessing to me because John admitted that HOT FLASHES ARE REAL AND HE FINALLY UNDERSTOOD WHY I HATED MENOPAUSE! Every time anyone mentioned that he was due for another injection, he would beg them to give him a break! (Lupron also has many other side affects that are very unpleasant for both husbands and wives, so the hot flashes were NOT the worst!)

It was a very long day by the time he got his first chemo treatment and a little after midnight when they released us. By the time we got home, he was sick as a dog. And he was that way all night long. We were supposed to be back at the medical center the next morning at 10, but around four o'clock in the morning I heard a horrible noise. I turned on the light as I called to him and he said, *"I got disoriented and fell into the bathtub."* When I got to the bathroom and turned on the light he was laying there in the tub covered in blood from a gash on his head and a huge gash on his thigh. I was shaking like a leaf and ran to call 911. He pleaded with me to just help him out of the tub because he had to go to the bathroom. He was 6'6" tall and weighed at that time about 250 pounds. I asked how I could possibly do that, and he said pray. I prayed and he was wobbly but he helped me get him out and to the potty. Just as he was going to sit down, he fell forward, hit the wall and in what seemed like slow motion, his head slid down the wall to the floor! I was crying out to God, "HELP ME, PLEASE GOD! YOU PROMISED NEVER TO LEAVE US OR FORSAKE US! I CAN'T MOVE HIM AND HE

IS FACE DOWN ON THE FLOOR! IT WASN'T SUPPOSED TO BE LIKE THIS! GOD PLEASE! I CAN'T EVEN LEAVE HIM TO CALL AN AMBULANCE—PLEASE GOD—I AM THANKFUL THAT *YOU ARE ABLE TO DO EXCEEDINGLY ABUNDANTLY MORE THAN I CAN ASK OR IMAGINE*—BUT I FEEL SO ALONE AND HELPLESS!" I also began to claim Psalm 46—"Lord you said you are my refuge and strength—a very present help in trouble and I don't have to fear!" Before I could take my next breath, I heard His still small voice say, "You are not alone—I promised I would never leave you nor forsake you. I am your help in times of trouble." I grabbed my John by the shoulders and tried to pull him away from the wall. He took a deep breath and said, "Count it all joy, Dian. Count it all JOY!" I was crying, blood was everywhere, his eyes were already turning black and his head and his leg had a gaping wound that would not stop bleeding. All he cared about was that he HAD TO GO TO THE BATHROOM! I helped him up, but it wasn't easy. He was slipping and sliding everywhere, and do you know what he said? "Where did all this blood come from?" I said, "Well there are only the two of us here, and from looking at you I'd say it wasn't me!" He looked at me sheepishly and said, "Are you sure? You're pretty bloody."

Count it all joy. You have GOT TO BE KIDDING ME! I AM STANDING IN THE MIDDLE OF WHAT LOOKS LIKE A CRIME SCENE—BOTH OF US COVERED IN BLOOD AND I'M TO COUNT IT ALL JOY? I didn't say that out loud, but trust me, that's what I was thinking. But while he was sitting in the bathroom, and I was listening to his concerto in B minor, I began to clean up the mess, and I began to sing "Great Is Thy Faithfulness". I listened to those lyrics as I sang them, and I began to praise Him that John had not died when he hit his head—once in the bathtub and once on the wall. I thanked God that I am a light sleeper, although I'm sure the neighbors heard the sickening noise of a 250-pound man falling into a sunken fiberglass tub. I thanked Him that I was only cleaning up blood at this point! And I thanked Him for giving John that beautiful verse, and that he remembered it the second he came to.

When James told us to "count it all joy" he used a word in the Greek that means facts, not feelings. According to Dave Anderson in his wonderful book *Triumph Through Trials,*[2] this scripture is saying, "be objective and don't let your feelings throw you in the midst of your trial. Get some perspective on this situation. Your feelings don't have to dictate joy." John always based things on fact while I went by feelings. I've prayed more than you can imagine that I would be a person who would get my feelings out of the way and rest on facts, knowing that God is sovereign, that no trial surprises Him, and nothing comes to you that He hasn't allowed to make you into the image of His precious Son. I firmly believe this trial was for my benefit because after this incident, I was able to say without doubt that nothing we went through was a surprise to God! Don't waste a thing you are going through. Lean hard on Him. Ask people to pray for you, and as you pray and have your friends and family pray, never forget that those prayers are going up to the THRONE OF GRACE—to the One Who created you, redeemed you, saved you, is sanctifying you and will one day come for you. HE LOVES YOU WITH AN EVERLASTING LOVE! HE IS ONE POWERFUL GOD!

LOOK AT THE SCRIPTURES:
[Eph. 3:20-21 NKJV] Now to Him who is able to do *exceedingly abundantly above all that we ask or think, according to the power that works in us,* to Him [be] glory in the church by Christ Jesus to all generations, forever and ever. Amen.

---

[2] Triumph through Trials: The Epistle of James; David R. Anderson, Grace Theology Press (2013)

OBSERVE THE MEANING OF THE WORDS "exceedingly" and "abundantly" and write them down.

VERIFY how they are being used in this scripture.

EXPLAIN how those words and that verse might help you or have helped you in a time of need.

Lord, You truly are all powerful and able to do exceeding and abundantly more than I could ever ask or imagine. Help me to remember that not only in the big things that come my way, but also in the small things when I don't even think to ask for help from You. You want me to depend on You and to call out to You in both.

MEET THE ADVERSARY

I'm sure there isn't a person reading this that doesn't remember the events of September 11, 2001. More than likely you can all remember exactly where you were that dreadful morning that America was attacked and so many people were killed—some never found because they were instantly incinerated. It didn't take long until our then President, George W. Bush, declared war on terrorism. The world has never been the same since that day. Flying has become more trouble than its worth; it's hard to trust anyone in an airport; it's scary to go to crowded places. You just never know when or where another attack will come. We live in a different world today thanks to the evil of terrorism. If you know what cancer is like, you know that when you hear the word, it doesn't take long until you realize you are in a war. Your life is never going to be the same again, just like our lives since 9/11 have never and will never be the same. But just as America's enemy has weapons of mass destruction—the enemy of our souls tries everything in his arsenal to steal, kill and destroy—from fear to confusion to anger to hatred and hopelessness and helplessness and back to fear again. I'm sure you realize I'm not just talking about our physical enemy, cancer. I'm talking about another enemy that can make this battle a thousand times worse. The enemy of our soul, Satan. He can make you feel defeated before you even start your day.

But I have some news for you—you can fight that enemy with THE WORD OF GOD! HOWEVER… *IF THE ENEMY CAN TAKE AWAY THE WORD OF GOD, HE HAS VICTORY! WHY? BECAUSE THAT'S WHERE YOUR POWER IS! That is important to remember because the battle of cancer, or any other trial you are facing, can be influenced by what you feed on.* I believe that is why the Holy Spirit gave both John and me *Scripture* every single day. **If the enemy can take away the Word of God, he can take from you the WORK of God.** You have a choice—either study and read the Word of God so that you know the God of the Word or don't.

Job was a man who very obviously knew God. [Job 1:1-12 NKJV] "There was a man in the land of Uz, whose name [was] Job; and that man was blameless and upright, and one who feared God and shunned evil. And seven sons and three daughters were born to him. Also, his possessions were seven thousand sheep, three thousand camels, five hundred yoke of oxen, five hundred female donkeys, and a very large household, so that this man was the greatest of all the people of the East. And his sons would go and feast [in their] houses, each on his [appointed] day, and would send and invite their three sisters to eat and drink with them. So it was, when the days of feasting had run their course, that Job would send and sanctify them, and he would rise early in the morning and offer burnt offerings [according to] the number of them all. For Job said, "It may be that my sons have sinned and cursed God in their hearts." Thus Job did regularly. Now there was a day when the sons of God came to present themselves before the LORD, and Satan also came among them. And the LORD said to Satan, "From where do you come?" So Satan answered the LORD and said, "From going to and fro on the earth, and from walking back and forth on it." Then the LORD said to Satan, "Have you considered My servant Job, that [there is] none like him on the earth, a blameless and upright man, one who fears God and shuns evil?" So Satan answered the LORD and said, "Does Job fear God for nothing? "Have You not made a hedge around him, around his household, and around all that he has on every side? You have blessed the work of his hands, and his possessions have increased in the land. "But now, stretch out Your hand and touch all that he has, and he will surely curse You to Your face!" And the LORD said to Satan, "Behold, all that he has [is] in your power; only do not lay a hand on his [person]." So Satan went out from the presence of the LORD."

In the first few verses of Job we are introduced to him and told a little about his family. He was a man of good character—he feared God and shunned evil. Scripture also says he was blameless and upright. In verses 2 and 3 we learn about his children—he was blessed with ten children and was very affluent. "And seven sons and three daughters were born to him. Also, his possessions were seven thousand sheep, three thousand camels, five hundred yoke of oxen, five hundred female donkeys, and a very large household, so that *this man was the greatest of all the people of the East."* Somehow I think those children must have had a wonderful childhood and really enjoyed being together because verses 4 and 5 we learn of his concern: *"… his sons would go and feast [in their] houses, each on his [appointed] day, and would send and invite their three sisters to eat and drink with them." "It may be that my sons have sinned and cursed God in their hearts."* Job cared more about God than anyone because he was described as upright and righteous, one who feared God and shunned evil AND wanted his sons and daughters to do the same. What a father and what a wonderful example of a godly man. Verse 5 says, "So it was, when the days of feasting had run their course, that Job would send and sanctify them, and he would rise early in the morning and offer burnt offerings [according to] the number of them all. For Job said, "It may be that my sons have sinned and cursed God in their hearts." Thus Job did regularly." To sanctify or consecrate means to set them apart or to cleanse. We can see examples of this in Gen. 36:2—"and Jacob said to his household and to all who were with him, "put away the foreign gods that are among you, purify yourselves, and change your garments!" Exodus 19:10 says, "Then the LORD said to Moses, "Go to the people and consecrate them today and tomorrow, and let them wash their clothes." And 1 Samuel 16:5—"And he said, 'Peaceably; I have come to sacrifice to the LORD. Sanctify your selves and come with me to the sacrifice.' Then he sanctified Jesse and his sons and invited them to the sacrifice."

Job, a man who feared God and shunned evil, even had the desire that his children would do the same. He was concerned that one of his children would knowingly or unknowingly curse God. Isn't this a beautiful example of praying for our children? I'm not sure there is anything more wonderful or powerful *we can do for them than to pray. Verse 5 says that Job rose early in the morning and offered burnt offerings according to the number of all!* Today, you and I offer up our prayers. We don't have to offer sacrifices because Jesus Christ was the perfect offering that sanctifies us. Today when we pray for our children, we know that the blood of Christ sanctifies them or sets them apart and cleanses them. If they do not know Christ, we ask that they be drawn to Him and would trust Him early in their lives. We "stand in the gap" for our children, interceding in prayer on their behalf. *James 5:16b says, "The effective, fervent prayer of a righteous man/woman avails much."*

Part of the story God has given me includes much prayer. I pray for my children and my grandchildren and through those prayers, God has worked miracles in their lives. I hope that everyone reading this believes in the power of prayer. Through the Word of God we learn how to know God, that it is through belief in His one and only Son, Jesus Christ. Through reading and studying the Word of God, we get to know Him personally and intimately! Another way we get to know Him is by memorizing scripture so that when we need Him, the Holy Spirit recalls scriptures to our memory and we hear Him as our counselor. We begin to learn to trust Him through men and women in the Bible who have trusted Him long before us. Through prayer, we learn to trust Him to protect our loved ones, to heal them, to teach them, to save and sanctify them. I believe Job spent a lifetime praying for and being an example to his family. I believe that Job knew much about God's character, that God is omnipotent, omniscient and omnipresent. He knew that there is no one like Him. That He is sovereign, He is eternal, always good, always wise and always in control. I believe that Job knew that nothing came to him that God had not allowed. And it's through this beautiful book of Job's suffering that we hear the voice of God, the Creator of all things, speak to Job. To me, what God answers out of the whirlwind includes some of the most beautiful and most sobering words in the Bible.

John and I had learned the truth concerning God BEFORE cancer came on the scene, but it was certainly driven home as we continued our journey. Here is an entry from our CaringBridge page on December 3, 2010:

"First of all, God is good, all the time—all the time, God is good. We will never feel any other way concerning that truth. He is our comfort, our joy, our peace, our provider: "Yea tho we walk through the valley of the shadow of death, we will fear no evil—He is with us!" (Psalm 23) Secondary to that, John's cancer has indeed progressed to the bones. The main lesion is in his spine in the lower back. There is also one on the pelvis on the left side, one (original to the bone met) on his collar bone, and one in the middle spine. The one on the lower portion of the spine is the one causing all the pain in his thighs and shins. They will do more testing early next week, then radiate the one that is the largest on the lower spine and start him on chemo to relieve the pain. We know that this is not a cure—this is a measure that will at least bring some relief. So please know that while we are sad, we do not grieve as those with no hope. Please continue to pray for him. He got new pain meds today that will help (hopefully) take the edge off. Please continue to pray that we will bring Glory to God by choosing to be joyful in this, another trial. And pray for me and those who love him so, Scott and Courtney and all our grandchildren and our siblings will remember that this life is not all there is and that we will be comforted by the fact that we know they love us and they know that we love them. CONSIDER IT PURE JOY WHEN... even in this–God is good."

If you are reading this book, I hope that you are already anchored deep into His abiding love by being in the Word and through prayer, praise, worship and thanksgiving, and if not, that you will begin right now. Had John and I not known Him deeply and seen Him in every aspect of our lives, this battle with cancer would have done us in. We would have thought we had been blindsided and even perhaps blamed God. The study of Job certainly gave us a better understanding of where trials can come from. God called the angels into His presence— even a fallen angel. Every created being is under the sovereign authority of God. That fact is very important and very comforting to me. It reminds me that HE is in control, and HE is definitely mighty. Look at some of the last verses of Job; they are magnificent and well worth remembering when walking through physical, mental, emotional or even spiritual pain. Then the LORD answered Job out of the whirlwind, and said:

> *Job 38:2–41 "Who is this who darkens counsel by words without knowledge? Now prepare yourself like a man; I will question you, and you shall answer Me.*
>
> *Where were you when I laid the foundations of the earth? Tell Me, if you have understanding. Who determined its measurements? Surely you know! Or who stretched the line upon it? To what were its foundations fastened? Or who laid its cornerstone, When the morning stars sang together, And all the sons of God shouted for joy? Or who shut in the sea with doors, When it burst forth and issued from the womb; When I made the clouds its garment, And thick darkness*

its swaddling band; When I fixed My limit for it, And set bars and doors; When I said, This far you may come, but no farther, And here your proud waves must stop!' "Have you commanded the morning since your days began, And caused the dawn to know its place, That it might take hold of the ends of the earth, And the wicked be shaken out of it? It takes on form like clay under a seal, And stands out like a garment. From the wicked their light is withheld, And the upraised arm is broken. "Have you entered the springs of the sea? Or have you walked in search of the depths? Have the gates of death been revealed to you? Or have you seen the doors of the shadow of death? Have you comprehended the breadth of the earth? Tell Me, if you know all this. "Where is the way to the dwelling of light? And darkness, where is its place, That you may take it to its territory? That you may know the paths to its home? Do you know it, because you were born then, Or because the number of your days is great? "Have you entered the treasury of snow, Or have you seen the treasury of hail, Which I have reserved for the time of trouble, For the day of battle and war? By what way is light diffused, Or the east wind scattered over the earth? "Who has divided a channel for the overflowing water, Or a path for the thunderbolt, To cause it to rain on a land where there is no one, A wilderness in To satisfy the desolate waste, And cause to spring forth the growth of tender grass? Has the rain a father? Or who has begotten the drops of dew?

From whose womb comes the ice? And the frost of heaven, who gives it birth? The waters harden like stone, And the surface of the deep is frozen. "Can you bind the cluster of the Pleiades, Or loose the belt of Orion? Can you bring out Mazzarothfn in its season? Or can you guide the Great Bear with its cubs? Do you know the ordinances of the heavens? Can you set their dominion over the earth? "Can you lift up your voice to the clouds, That an abundance of water may cover you? Can you send out lightnings, that they may go, And say to you, 'Here we are!'? Who has put wisdom in the mind? Or who has given understanding to the heart? Who can number the clouds by wisdom? Or who can pour out the bottles of heaven, When the dust hardens in clumps, And the clods cling together? "Can you hunt the prey for the lion, Or satisfy the appetite of the young lions, When they crouch in their dens, Or lurk in their lairs to lie in wait? Who provides food for the raven, When its young ones cry to God, And wander about for lack of food?

There is only one answer to any of those questions—YOU, OH LORD! YOU ALONE! We don't know what's going on in the heavens. Getting to know Him BEFORE trials come keeps us from being battered and torn in the storms of life. *1 Peter 1:3-8 says it best — "we have a living hope through the resurrection of Jesus Christ. A hope that doesn't fade away…though now for a little while, if need be, you have been grieved by various trials…that the genuineness of your faith…though tested by fire, may be found to praise, honor, and glory at the revelation of Jesus Christ!"* Your faith will be tested, but if your faith is in God, you can trust that He is sovereign and still on the Throne. You can trust Him to handle whatever may come your way.

A great example of knowing Scripture in a time of need is this account that happened in the middle of our cancer experience: I took John into MDACC this morning for IV fluids, and he had lost a little over 11 pounds since Tuesday afternoon. He was in pain and very dehydrated due to all the nausea. He was unable to keep down anything, most especially his pain meds. I got dressed and told him we were going to the hospital immediately. He said he was unable to get there so I told him that was no problem–that I would call 911. He "miraculously" got up, slowly but up, and I dressed him and took him in. They took one look at him and put him in a bed in the infusion suite, started IV fluids, pain meds, steroids, etc. His oncologist told him that if he wasn't better in a couple of hours, she would admit him. He was a little low on platelets and low on potassium. I asked her how I could manage his pain since he couldn't keep the meds down, and she wrote a script for a pain patch. It will take the place of the oxycontin 12-hour time release tablets. He is now able to keep down Dilaudid every four hours. We arrived home this afternoon. He showered and sat outside for a while and went back to bed around 5:30. Eiley (our eldest granddaughter) is here from San Angelo, and she, together with Hope and Courtney, came over for a few hours. They did a world of good for Kemosabe. He hated to tell them that he was going to bed, but they were happy he was honest.

Last night after two suppositories for nausea, he finally settled down enough to get a little rest from 4 or 5 a.m. until around 7. I lay there after he finally slept and recalled Isaiah 26:3, "You will keep him in perfect peace, Whose mind is stayed on You, Because he trusts in You." I began to reflect on God's faithfulness throughout the Bible and I realized that the same God who was with Adam and Eve, Noah, Moses, Daniel, etc., is the same God who is with me and with John— even closer because He isn't leading by a pillar of fire or a cloud, but rather He, by the power of His Holy Spirit, indwells me and John. He is closer than our breath, closer than a heartbeat. Needless to say, I was peacefully sleeping before I got to the account of Joshua, which is long before Daniel—and I was so looking forward to remembering Shadrach, Meshach and Abednigo, not to mention Daniel in that lions' den!

Three generations of Sustek men (2008)

Five of the magnificent seven grands

44th Anniversary Dinner (August 2011)

45th Anniversary

Family Photo Session (March 2013)
Front Row – Jon, Carson, Devyn, Hope
Back Row – John, Dian, Paige

Family photo session (March 2013)
Courtney, Dian, John, and Scott

Family Thanksgiving (2011)
Back row: John, Greg, Scott;   Middle Row: Karen, Dian, Paula,
Courtney (holding Hope), Eiley, Mia, Kay;
Front row: Meyer (with Jon in his lap), Devyn

Beginning of hospice (June 2013)

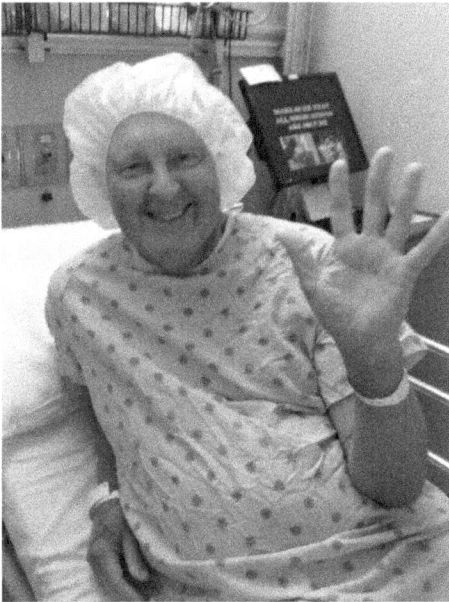

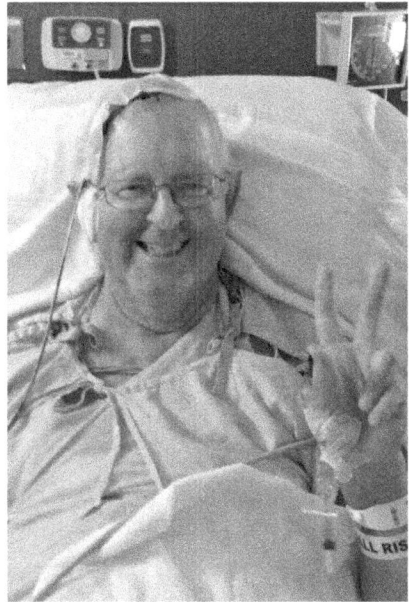

Kemosabe before and after 12 ½ hour flap surgery (September 2011)

Jon saying goodbye to Abba (July 2013)

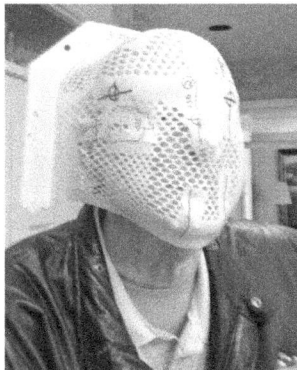

Intense brain radiation (2013)

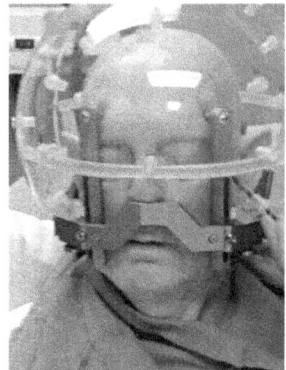

Intense brain radiation (2013)

LOOK AT THE VERSES FROM JOB 1:1-5.

OBSERVE WHO IS PRIMARILY MENTIONED.

VERIFY USING PARALLEL VERSES.

EXAMPLES OF OTHERS IN THE BIBLE WHO WERE OF GOOD CHARACTER.

LOOK AT YOUR LIFE and make a list of friends or family members that may have this sort of character. Perhaps you have an upright, godly character. Perhaps you need improvement. Let's face it, we can all make improvements, and if we pray about those things we would like to improve, the Holy Spirit will help us to be able to do so. Philippians 4:13 tells us that, "we can do ALL THINGS through Christ who strengthens us."

Father God, please let me never forget that I CAN do all things through Christ Jesus. He is my strength and my salvation. Lord, I never want to stop running to Your Word to find answers because I want to remember that if the evil one can take away Your Word, he can also affect Your work in me.

BE JOYFUL ALWAYS

Rejoice always, pray without ceasing, in everything give thanks; for this is the will of God in Christ Jesus for you. 1 Thess. 5:16-18

I love these verses. When we lived in Miami, they were the first verses I memorized. Why? Because I was grumpy and hated it there. Oh, it was a beautiful place to live—but at that time, integration of schools was just being instituted in Florida. Not sure why it was so slow to arrive, but it involved children from our neighborhood being bused to a neighborhood far away. It was difficult enough for Courtney, then in elementary school, to begin a new school. We had lived in Pondcrosa Forest and were close enough to walk to school. All of her friends had been her friends since kindergarten—even preschool—and they all lived in our neighborhood! Now she was to be bused across town? An hour each way? I don't think so. And on top of that, NO ONE TOLD US ABOUT THIS or we would never have bought a home where we did! But God knew, and He worked things out. There was a little private church school not far from our home, and that's where she went for two years. That's also where the neighborhood children went, and they all became very close friends in a very short amount of time. And the best part? She learned and memorized Scripture and put it into practice and she loved it! I'm not sure how we afforded it, but looking back, I don't remember doing without anything. Thank you, Lord, for your lovingkindness.

Why do you suppose that it's God's will for us to follow those instructions? I say "instructions" because they aren't suggestions. In context of this letter to the Thessalonians, Paul is telling them that the day of the Lord will come like a thief in the night! He wanted them (and us) to be awake and alert and to put on faith and love as a breastplate and the hope of salvation as a helmet. He was telling them (and us) to guard our hearts (faith and love as our breastplate) and minds (hope of salvation as a helmet) because we who are His are not going to suffer His wrath but receive salvation through our Lord Jesus Christ! THAT'S why we can be joyful—we will never suffer the wrath of God! We need to keep an eternal perspective whatever we go through here on earth because this isn't our final destination! Focusing on that truth and praying and thanking Him not only gets our minds off ourselves and our problems, it puts everything into the right perspective. And I can tell you from experience that you can and you WILL BE JOYFUL when your eyes are on the prize! Many many days and nights, I sang songs of worship and praise to John when he was in pain. I put hymns and praise music on the CD player and we sang along with them. He would fall into a deep sleep every single time. I tell you this because it's true and because you need to know that there is great power in the Word of God. God wants to do a work in you and through you. Remember He is creating you into the image of His Son, Jesus Christ, and He is writing His story on your heart!

I want to give you some examples of what can happen when others observe you being joyful and praying and giving thanks in all circumstances. People at MDACC would approach us and ask if we were visiting someone at the hospital. When John would tell them that HE had cancer, they would stand there with their mouths hanging open! They would tell us their stories and then ask how we did what we did—how could we be so joyful going through such trials and for so long. John would ask, "Are you a Christian?" If they said "yes," he would give them our life scriptures. We would pray with them and tell them our story—abbreviated. If they said "no," then we would witness to them and talk about living above our circumstances because this world is not all there is. Some would walk away from us, but most would listen and say that sounded wonderful but not for them OR they would trust Christ. I was always glad when someone would tell us that they had tried religion, but it wasn't really that great because it was all about following rules. I was glad because I could explain that having Christ in me was my hope of glory! That what we had was NOT RELIGION! Then we could talk about a relationship with Jesus Christ who came to seek and save the lost! That He was Messiah to the Jews, the One they had waited for and looked for! And that because of His great love for His creation, we as Gentiles are grafted into the Jewish people.

One day while John was having a CT scan, I was waiting in a very crowded room when a Rabbi signed in and asked if he had time to get something to eat or drink. The lady at the desk said he was already late, and he explained his flight from NYC was late. She wasn't very nice, and he just sat down. He looked so sick, and my heart just broke for him. I walked over to him and said, "Sir, I know right where the cafeteria is, and I'd be happy to go get you something. What would you like?" He was shocked and said, "Oh, I couldn't put you to that trouble." I told him it was no trouble at all and that all he had to do was tell me what he wanted. He was stunned but said he would love a coke and perhaps a sandwich. I told him I'd be right back, and when I returned he was still there, looking very pale and shaking. I gave him the food. He asked me to wait so he could pay me but I said, "No sir—please just accept it as a gift in the name of Jesus Christ. He is the One who provides all things. Blessings to you in His Name." He stared at me, and they called his name. He kept staring at me as he walked into the back for them to take his vitals. I never saw him again as John came out soon. We prayed for him when we got in the car. I sure hope his eyes were opened that day or soon after because there he was, a man for whom Christ came—who has the Old Testament and hasn't recognized that Messiah has come and he is loved. Throughout the Old Testament there are pictures of Christ—each feast pointing the Jews to their Messiah. Somehow in those few moments I had with him, I found a deep love for that man I believe it was God's love. I still pray for him to this day. I'll never forget his face.

I could go on and on about our experiences there they included doctors and nurses, technicians. After eight years, trust me... almost everyone both at the main campus and out at the satellite campus in The Woodlands knew we were Christians and knew our story. When John went on to glory, many of those people came to his celebration of life. And in November, when Grace School Of Theology had their banquet that John had planned, MDACC filled a table with doctors and nurses that had treated him. I can't tell you how many people we prayed with and for in those eight years, but I do know that no prayer goes unanswered. And I'll tell you something else—because God had instructed us to pray continually, our eyes were outward focused—not on ourselves or our circumstances. It seemed that every visit was kind of like going to church. We worshipped, we prayed and we fellowshipped with other believers. There were many times that we would even see friends there that were going through the same fight we were walking. Those were such treats from God! There were also many times we would laugh ourselves silly while at the hospital, whether it was for treatments or just appointments for scans. One that I remember clearly was at the end of the third round of chemo, while he was laying in bed waiting for vitals, I noticed a rogue eyebrow. It was one that I was always plucking or trimming for as long as we'd been married and it bugged him to death that it bugged me! Anyhow, due to my chin hairs and his wild brow, I always had tweezers in my purse. So I plucked that wild eyebrow hair and on the way home, he ran his hand though his hair and a huge wad came out! He said it was my fault because I plucked the eyebrow that was holding in all his hair! We both laughed, but then went straight to the hair dresser and he had her shave his head. A week later, my hair started falling out! I said to him, "Listen, I'm getting sick of being nauseous when you are and having diarrhea when you do! I even have pain in my legs and back when you do! BUT LOSING MY HAIR? THAT'S THE LIMIT, BUSTER!" We both laughed about that, but I bought a wig!

...be joyful always, pray continually, give thanks in all things —why? because this is God's will for you in Christ Jesus!

LOOK AT THE WORD JOYFUL
What does the word JOYFUL mean? Does it depend on your circumstances? Does it come naturally?

OBSERVE HOW IT'S USED IN SCRIPTURE.

VERIFY IT WITH OTHER SCRIPTURE.

EXAMPLES OF OTHERS IN SCRIPTURE EXHIBITING JOY.

Oh, Lord Jesus—YOU are able to pour joy into my heart even in the most desperate situations. Therefore we also, since we are surrounded by so great a cloud of witnesses, let us lay aside every weight, and the sin which so easily ensnares us, and let us run with endurance the race that is set before us, looking unto Jesus, the author and finisher of our faith, who for the joy that was set before Him endured the cross, despising the shame, and has sat down at the right hand of the throne of God.

LIFE AND CANCER GOES ON

The Lord your God is with you, He is mighty to save He will take great delight in you—in ME—He will quiet you with HIS LOVE, He will rejoice over you with singing! Zeph. 3:17

From 2005 until 2013, John had many metastases. His cancer progressed from the prostate to the lymph nodes to the bones to the lungs and lastly to the brain. That's the one I can truly say I hated the most. He was a brilliant man with three degrees from Rice University in mechanical and aerospace engineering. He had many patents and spoke several languages. His thesis for his Ph.D. had to do with designing the tiles that would keep the space shuttle cool during re-entry to the earth's atmosphere. But his proudest accomplishment cost him nothing—his salvation by Jesus Christ and his decision to become His disciple, which cost him everything as discipleship does. It is the sanctification process. He was serious about his love for Jesus and everyone knew it. We had prayed for a way to give God glory, and this was God's answer to that prayer. Suffering. This would be our open letter to the world that God is real and that Jesus Christ came in the flesh and left His Holy Spirit to show others that indeed, we can do all things though Christ who strengthens us.

For many months God had blessed us with relatively good health for John, meaning remission for weeks and months at a time. On September 1, 2011, after many tests and lots of biopsies on a tumor on his head, John endured a twelve hour operation for a leiomyosarcoma (LMS) on his head. LMS is a deadly cancer that can only be treated by removing every cell. It does not respond to chemo or radiation. I looked back on my journal, and this is what I had posted when we found the results of this biopsy. "This is a very nasty cancer and we ask again that you pray for John and our family as we face once again another type of cancer. We decided on the way home from MDACC that compared to this, prostate cancer had probably been a walk in the park. John told me after hearing the news, that he is no longer concerned about the stock market or the terrible Texas drought! God certainly has a way of putting things into perspective! There is nothing we need more right now than prayer for we know that "all things work together for good for those who love God—for those who are called according to HIS PURPOSE—and that purpose is that He is creating us into the image of His Son. Therefore, again—we rejoice in this, another trial, and count on His great mercy, and we consider this new challenge part of His marvelous grace."

This surgery was twelve grueling hours long and one week afterward, the "flap" was showing signs of dying so they whisked him back into surgery to try to save it. Another ten hours in surgery, and it was too hard on his heart. He had a heart attack on the table. Prayers flooded heaven. Doctors and nurses of faith flooded his room in CICU. You could feel the presence of the Lord in that place.

John's sister, Karen, was there, Courtney, myself, Scott and our eldest granddaughter, Eiley, were there. It was very obvious that we were not alone. But for some reason, I *felt* very much alone. There was no reason for me to feel that way, but looking back, I think I felt as though God for some reason hadn't heard my prayers—probably just because of stress and yes, another challenge. I'll be honest—I was growing weary of one more challenge—one more surprise—one more trial. My heart knew the truth, but my mind was wearing out. I left the room and went down to the chapel. I cried out to God how I felt—A L O N E ! ! ! Zeph 3:17 "The Lord your God is with you, He is nighty to save He will take great delight in you—in ME—He will quiet you with HIS LOVE, He will rejoice over you with singing!" Psalm 73:23–26—"I am always with you—you hold me by my right hand—you guide me with your counsel and afterward you will take me into glory. whom have I in heaven but you? My flesh and my heart may fail, but God is the strength of my heart and my portion forever!" He reminded me I was NEVER ALONE, but I told Him that's how I felt. He then reminded me I had taken my eyes off HIM AND HIS WORD and put them on the circumstances! I read and re-read those passages from Scripture and I purposed in my heart to keep my focus on HIM—THE author and finisher of my faith and NOT ON TEMPORARY CIRCUMSTANCES! I left the chapel and got on elevator C. If you know anything about MDACC, every elevator has a letter or a number and they are color coded. Trust me, that's a good thing because you don't want to get on the wrong elevator as there was no telling where you'd end up! It's a regular city down there! There was only one other person on it, which was a miracle as they are all usually crowded—a man who turned to me and said, "Do I know you?" I said, "Aren't you Terry Teykl?" He replied, "Yes"—we then realized God had sent him at that exact time to remind me that HE IS STILL IN CONTROL AND I AM NEVER ALONE! At that time, I had only met Terry once and that was at my sister's house about a month or so before John's surgery. Terry is a great prayer warrior and the chaplain for Christian Radio Station KSBJ in Houston, Texas. He went with me to John's room in CICU and prayed with and for us and sat with us for awhile. From that moment on, I never felt like I was alone. God had sent me His reminder that day on elevator C that He hears my prayers and knows my needs.

Do you ever feel alone in your struggles and pain? You are NEVER ALONE if you know Jesus Christ! He promises never to leave you or forsake you. I love Psalm 56:3-4—*"Whenever I am afraid I will trust in you—in God I will praise His Word—in God I have put my trust; I will not fear. What can flesh do to me?"* Please practice keeping your eyes off your circumstances and putting them on our GREAT AND AWESOME GOD! Get into His Word and read it every single day. If you're not already in a Bible study, I encourage to you either join one or begin one on your own. Your weapons of mass destruction are not physical weapons. They are literally GOD'S WORD!

Let me remind you—if the enemy can take away the Word of God, he can take away the WORK of God—DON'T LET THAT HAPPEN!

LOOK AT THE SCRIPTURE
Zephaniah 3:17—*The Lord your God is with you, He is mighty to save He will take great delight in you—in ME—He will quiet you with HIS LOVE,* **He will rejoice over you with singing!**

OBSERVE the phrase—HE WILL QUIET YOU WITH HIS LOVE.

VERIFY how He has comforted you in the past.

EXPLAIN in your own words a time when you realized He took delight in you.

Heavenly Father, I thank You that I am never alone. I thank You that when I am FEELING alone, You send someone to show me that I am NEVER alone. Thank You that even when I feel alone, Your Spirit is always with me and always guides me to where I need to go. Thank You that You rejoice over me with singing!

THE LOSS OF A LOVED ONE

"For My thoughts are not your thoughts, Nor are your ways My ways," says the LORD. "For as the heavens are higher than the earth, So are My ways higher than your ways, And My thoughts than your thoughts." Is. 55:9-13

At the same time John was going through his battle with cancer, my sister Paula's husband was deteriorating from a disease called CIPD—a progressive disorder that mimics ALS. He had been in a wheelchair for two or three years by Thanksgiving and had never given up hope of walking again. Meyer and Paula had gotten married a year or so after me and John, and we were all quite close. Meyer had been diagnosed with CIPD in 2008, and we had all watched as he tried everything his doctors suggested to try and reverse the toll this was taking on his body. After Thanksgiving dinner in 2012, while dessert was being served, Meyer announced that he would be having surgery on his neck because they had determined that he had spinal stenosis. He was hopeful that once that was taken care of, he would walk again. He knew it would take time and a lot of physical therapy, but he was willing to go through anything to walk again. We were all so happy for him. He was just ecstatic, and his whole countenance was better than it had been in months, maybe even years. We prayed that this would bring healing to our brother. He had always been a very jovial man. Everyone loved Meyer! He was caring, generous, and very physical! We were, as he was, looking forward to him being able to walk through the door with a huge smile and make us all laugh again! Of course, he still made us laugh. Nothing stopped his great sense of humor, but oh how he looked forward to walking again.

On December 13, 2012, at around 4:30 or five o'clock in the morning, my sister, Paula, got a call that she needed to get to the hospital immediately. She was staying at a friend's home in the Medical Center and just had to run across the bridge to the Methodist Hospital. When she got to his room, he was already gone. It was the most shockingly tragic day we had faced so far in all these years of our marriage. Of course Paula was devastated, but I had never seen John so stricken and broken over anything. He KNEW he was dying. He had known since 2005. But Meyer, no one, not one doctor had ever said that his illness would lead to death. The surgery had nothing to do with it–an autopsy revealed that information. It took John several weeks to come to grips with the fact that while we were all shocked by this turn of events, God was not. It had been easy for John to accept his own mortality, but Meyer was another story. He did, however, finally come to terms with God's sovereign plan when he remembered the toll Meyer's illness had taken on him and how he never wanted to be a quadriplegic. There had been a possibility that he could have been, had the surgery not gone well. John began to come to the conclusion that indeed, God had been merciful and taken Meyer home perhaps in order to spare him a lifetime of living in a body that had entrapped him.

God's grace comes in many different forms. We tend to think that His grace is to heal and to allow everything to go our way. But God's grace entails much more than doing things our way. *Psalm 145:17—"The LORD is righteous in all His ways, Gracious in all His works. Romans 11:33—"Oh, the depth of the riches both of the wisdom and knowledge of God! How unsearchable are His judgments and His ways past finding out!*

I was reading in Isaiah while studying one day, and these verses hit me as being a word concerning God's grace. These words were written to Israel but are fitting for Meyer's life and those of us who knew him well. *Isa 55:8-13. "For My thoughts are not your thoughts, Nor are your ways My ways," says the LORD "For as the heavens are higher than the earth, So are My ways higher than your ways, And My thoughts than your thoughts. "For as the rain comes down, and the snow from heaven, And do not return there, But water the earth, And make it bring forth and bud, That it may give seed to the sower And bread to the eater, So shall My word be that goes forth from My mouth; It shall not return to Me void, But it shall accomplish what I please And it shall prosper in the thing for which I sent it, "For you shall go out with joy, And be led out with peace; The mountains and the hills Shall break forth into singing before you, And all the trees of the field shall clap their hands. Instead of the thorn shall come up the cypress tree, And instead of the brier shall come up the myrtle tree; And it shall be to the LORD for a name, For an everlasting sign that shall not be cut off."*

Even when we are close to Christ and know Him well, there are times when we feel hurt and disappointed and we wonder, why? Why would He take this person away? Why would He not heal him after all the prayers and all the hope? Why would He decide to take a life rather than to deliver him from death? All the whys seem to overcome us and we fall into despair and depression. But if we can get our minds and hearts back to TRUTH, we find the answers. The problem is that our default is usually to question or to fear or to blame. That's human nature.

God is always good. He never changes. He always has our good and His glory in mind above our wants. Death is not all there is! He has a life that no one can imagine—a home that we cannot fathom—

waiting for us on the other side! Our problem comes when we can't see past the end of the day, or even the end of the next five minutes! God wants us to have a different perspective, one that is eternal so that even when what we consider to be the worst happens, He can show us there is another way. Another world. Another kingdom! None of us knows when we will breathe our last breath on this side of eternity. We don't have a clue when anyone we love will either! Sure we may have been told that we have a fatal illness—but really, no one other than God knows when our time will come. So why not live our lives in such a way that when that happens, we are not only prepared to say goodbye to those we love in this world but are also ready to run to Jesus in the next?

LOOK AT PSALM 145:17 and write out the most important words YOU see in those verses.

OBSERVE THE WAY those words comfort you.

VERIFY that Scripture with Romans 11:33 and compare how they both bring comfort.

EXPLAIN a time when you might have questioned God on these TRUTHS!

Sweet Lord, the loss of someone close to us is a very deep hurt, most especially when it is not expected. Help me to remember that nothing surprises You and that those who have put their trust in You are never lost—only waiting on the other side for us to fellowship with them once more. Thank You that You are righteous in all Your ways and gracious in all Your works. Thank You that You are near to all who call upon You, to all who call upon You in truth.

CHRISTMAS AND THE NEW YEAR

1 Peter 3:8... joy inexplicable

God gave us Christmas of 2012 with relatively normal health for John, at least he was feeling good enough to celebrate Christmas in San Angelo with all of our children and most of the grands. That Christmas carried a heaviness since Meyer had died just two weeks before, but we tried to focus on the birth of Christ—the very reason for the season. But January and February of 2013 were full of more suffering than we could've ever imagined. I can honestly tell you that I don't remember most of those two months because we were immersed in the Word of God as we traveled back and forth for treatment—thankfully in The Woodlands. He took many radiation treatments on his brain because the tumors were multiplying so quickly. We would come home from his treatment, and he would immediately go to bed. At this point, nothing seemed to stop this invading monster. We both knew the time was near, but the thought for me was almost unbearable. We continued enjoying our family and friends and continued our little treks to MDACC until June.

But on February 12, 2013, John awakened around eight o'clock that morning and declared; "JOY! JOY HAS DESCENDED ON

ME! IT'S TRUE—JOY HAS DESCENDED AND I FEEL THE PRESENCE OF JESUS AND HIS JOY!" He also said that God had compelled him to do three things—

1. Pray without ceasing for me, his wife.
2. Read the Bible all day and whenever he was awake at night.
3. Tell everyone he came in contact with about Jesus.

1 Peter 1:3-8—"BLESSED BE THE GOD AND FATHER OF OUR LORD JESUS CHRIST, WHO ACCORDING TO HIS ABUNDANT MERCY HAS BEGOTTEN US AGAIN TO A LIVING HOPE THROUGH THE RESURRECTION OF JESUS CHRIST FROM THE DEAD, TO AN INHERITANCE INCORRUPTIBLE AND UNDEFILED AND THAT DOES NOT FADE AWAY RESERVED IN HEAVEN FOR YOU, WHO ARE KEPT BY THE POWER OF GOD THROUGH FAITH FOR SALVATION READY TO BE REVEALED IN THE LAST TIME! IN THIS YOU GREATLY REJOICE, THOUGH NOW, FOR A LITTLE WHILE, IF NEED BE, YOU HAVE BEEN GRIEVED BY VARIOUS TRIALS.......*THAT THE GENUINENESS OF YOUR FAITH BEING MUCH MORE PRECIOUS THAN GOLD THAT PERISHES, THOUGH IT IS TESTED BY FIRE; MAY BE FOUND TO PRAISE, HONOR AND GLORY AT THE REVELATION OF JESUS CHRIST, WHOM HAVING NOT SEEN YOU LOVE. THOUGH NOW YO DO NOT SEE HIM, YET BELIEVING YOU REJOICE WITH JOY INEXPRESSIBLE AND FULL OF GLORY!* That verse came alive for John. This is the entry I put on our CaringBridge page after this wonderful miracle from God:

JOY DESCENDS, Feb 26, 2013, 4:57 p.m.

So sorry I haven't updated this or our CaringBridge page! But here I am and hang on 'cause it's been a wild ride! John took his last radiation treatment yesterday. As you know, the ones on his brain were completed on the fifth or sixth of February, but that very afternoon, they began radiation on his lower back for a tumor that was causing a great deal of pain. Now that those have been eradicated we hope—the doctors have decided to give him four weeks off and at the end of that time, he will go in for scans to see how things are looking. Pain is a huge indicator of more mets and at the present time, he is pain free which is a blessing of the greatest magnitude! We are praising God for His mercies towards us and for the healing touch He has given through our doctors. Thank you all so much for your sweet prayers. They have been heard and answered in wonderful ways.

The most wonderful thing that has come of all of this is that today begins the third week of the most inexplicable joy John has ever experienced in his life. He says he is joyful when he is laying in bed, even if he can't sleep; joyful waking up each morning, joyful doing anything and everything and that it is the most powerful thing he can imagine. He says he believes that the Lord has given him a foretaste of the joy that is to come when in heaven his joy will be complete! What an awesome gift from God, not only to him, but to our family for it will be such a comforting thing to remember when the time comes for him to be absent from the body and present with the Lord! (Not that I am looking forward to that day, but at least I will remember this time and what God has done for him!)

Thank you for you consistent, persistent, expectant prayers! We love you all!

LOOK AT 1 PETER 1:3-8 in two or three versions.
OBSERVE WHO IS KEEPING OUR INHERITANCE.

VERIFY THE FACT THAT WE CAN BE GRIEVED AND REJOICE AT THE SAME TIME!

EXPLAIN A TIME WHEN PERHAPS YOU FELT GRIEF AND JOY TOGETHER.

My Lord Jesus, You and only You can understand what John and I felt on that day when we read and re-read those verses from 1 Peter! Indeed You gave John JOY INEXPLICABLE that overflowed from his heart and his body to most everyone who came in contact with him. It was YOUR JOY, Lord. Joy that flowed from the promises You gave him in Christ Jesus. What a beautiful witness he was for your glory. Thank you that my sweet family and I were witnesses of that miracle.

GAMMA KNIFE

Matthew 11:28...come to Me, all you who labor and are heavy laden, and I will give you rest.

June was an obvious downward trend where John fought for his life, even including a gamma knife procedure to remove three tumors in his brain that were doubling in size every 48 hours. There was no way John's life would be able to continue on this earth, and after asking the Lord to give us wisdom—since James 1 tells us that if we lack wisdom we can ask of God and HE WILL GIVE IT— John finally realized that his time on earth and our time together was short. He wanted what time he had left to be spent with his family and closest friends, and he wanted every minute to count for eternity. He and I also learned the lessons that JOB had learned—that

- Suffering is a great equalizer
- Suffering makes us dependent on God and others
- Suffering changes our focus
- Suffering humbles the proud
- Suffering helps distinguish between necessities and luxuries
- Suffering teaches us patience

- Suffering teaches us the difference between valid fear and exaggerated fear
- Suffering brings the gospel into focus and brings HOPE and COMFORT
- Suffering allows us to respond to the gospel with abandonment and uncomplicated totality because we have so little to lose!

This is an abbreviated list from Philip Yancey's great book, [3] *Where Is God When It Hurts?* And through personal experience, I have to say that in every instance, they are true. Those are the times you begin to realize that not only is Jesus with you, but He is also holding you. He is ministering to you. He gives you strength, and He gives you boldness. He comforts you, and in answer to Philip Yancey's question, WHERE IS GOD WHEN IT HURTS—HE IS WITH YOU!

After the gamma knife surgery, John and I walked out of the hospital. He was supposed to spend the night, but somehow he was lost in the shuffle in the surgical waiting area. After laying there for nine hours, he said, "Dian, get my walker, a wheelchair and my things. We are going home." That was my evidence that John was through with medical help. He and I laid in bed that night and listened to Vince Gill sing "THREATEN ME WITH HEAVEN." That had become John's favorite song and kind of a theme for him. However, he resisted Hospice because he felt it was selfish to leave his family. He had spoken with his doctors, nurses and friends, but as long as even one person said they MIGHT be able to do one more thing, he would cling to life in that pain-ridden body of death. Scott called our dear friend, Jack Lesch, who had retired from his practice and joined Hospice in order to help those who were ready to finish the race. Jack came over and simply said to John, "Friend, you have fought the good

---

[3] Where is God When it Hurts; Philip Yancey Zondervan Publishing House

fight for a long, long time. Don't you think it's time to rest?" Rest. The key word John needed to hear. *Matthew 11:29-30–"Take My yoke upon you and learn from Me, for I am gentle and lowly in heart, and you will find rest for your souls. "For My yoke is easy and My burden is light."* Exactly what John needed to hear.

On June 18, 2013, at 11:28 a.m., John made the very brave decision to choose the rest of Hospice over the rigors of treatment. He had fought the good fight for the past almost nine years, and the time had come when God had a better plan—a time of rest, a time of family and friends, a time where he could be home and enjoy the blessings of this life before entering into the TRUE REST OF ETERNAL LIFE! We were in the thankful, sad, joyful, expectant, new kind of normal mode, and we cherished all prayers as we moved from day to day, knowing that each day that passed was one day closer to having to say goodbye for only a little while. Jesus has promised that He goes to prepare a place for us and that when the time is right, He will take us to that place. We knew that John/Abba would rejoice and be glad when he saw his Savior face to face! And we knew that we would be sad to have to see him go—but we would always remember the joy that was set before him and descended on him from February until the day he left this world! Thank you all for caring for us so well. And thank you, Jack Lesch, for reminding us all that this is a time of rest.

Here is a message I posted on our Facebook page that afternoon: "My sweet John, our children's 'daddy' and our grandchildren's Abba made the decision this afternoon not to continue treatment for his cancer. I imagined this time would be far away and that when the time came, I would feel a sense of relief for him and for his suffering. I was wrong. While I hate the suffering, I am so sad I can't stand myself. Whatever will I do without the man I have loved since I was 19 years old? Please God, give me the strength I need to get through whatever comes next. You have filled us with YOUR JOY, YOUR PEACE and YOUR STRENGTH for the past nine years, but tonight

I feel sick and sad and lonely and hurt and like I can't take another breath. Please God, give me and our children and grandchildren what we need minute by minute. And above all else, please give John your mercy and a vision of what You have promised him. We who were in the room could see him physically relax."

The time had come to get ready to go home. Realizing that our time was short John wanted to spend every minute doing all he could to have what time was left count for eternity. He spent hours and hours with our family and close friends, leaving us with words of encouragement and instructions. He reminded me of his final wishes concerning his cremation. Not one thing was left undone or unsaid. In fact, this is a good time to interject a very practical but important thing—a gift actually that John did during these last two weeks. I pray that this will be of help to anyone who may be going through the approaching death of a loved one. John called his sweet friend, Kyle Mays, to come and see him. He and Kyle fished together and Kyle's dad, John, also fished with my John. Kyle also happened to be our investment counselor. After being with Kyle for a while in the bedroom, John called me in and said to me, "Dian, go with Kyle and do whatever he tells you to do." I said, "What is he going to tell me to do?" He said, "Just please go with him and do whatever he says." It was now time to exercise my power of attorney. I shook all over and told John, "I can't! I just can't! You are still here! Please don't make me do that!" He said, "Honey, when I die, it will be too late. Please do as I say. This is what I want." I cried for days after that. Not in front of him, but it just made everything so real—so terribly real. Several weeks later when I met with my attorney, he said to me, "Do you realize that by John having you exercise that power of attorney, he gifted you everything? In other words, you will not pay tax on any of that money." It took many weeks for that to sink in to my feeble brain. And in fact, I'm still amazed at the kindness and the wisdom of God in every area of my life at that time.

All of our children and grandchildren came and stayed and sat with him, and we all talked and read from the Bible. Not once in the 2 1/2 weeks was there not hymns and praise music playing. (Well to be honest, there was a day or so that he wanted to hear songs from the sixties, and we all sang along and danced in the bedroom!) He was weak as a kitten, but he wiggled around in that bed and enjoyed himself. Everyone who entered that bedroom felt the presence of the Lord. There was a constant parade of friends and family members going in and out of the house saying their goodbyes. In fact, one guy came so many times that John said to him, "Hey buddy—I've counted at least five goodbyes from you!" I thank God that He waited until July to take John home. School was out and we were all able to be there. Sweet Erin, or "Erin the Cutie" as John called her, took off from her busy schedule as a neonatal nurse in San Angelo. Our daughter, Courtney, lived only a few miles from us, and she was over every single day. They all spent the nights at our home so that we could all be there for Abba, as the grands all called him. We all clung to every breath he took, knowing that the last would come at anytime. Dear friends, Gwen and Hack Kirkpatrick, who had brought more meals and spent more hours with us than anyone other than family, drove in from Dallas. They had lived in California and then in The Woodlands when we were there—over 20 years of friendship. We had gone through the good, the bad and the ugly with Gwen and Hack. We knew them as well as we knew one another. They moved to Dallas to be close to their grandsons the year before John died. But we knew they were only a phone call away. Glenn and Sherry Darby were often in our home during this time, praying with and praying over John and me. When John felt well enough, Glenn would take him on long drives, just to get him out into the fresh air. Before John was really bad, they would spend the day at Glenn's farm, fishing in John's favorite pond. It did John good and to be honest, me too! Scores of friends called and came to visit and pray. It never failed that when we felt the lowest, God would send someone we loved to come spend time with us.

One of the biggest blessings God bestowed on us during this time was when our dear friend and sister in Christ came over one afternoon, Dr. Margaret Nikol. Margaret is a world renowned violinist and speaks boldly in the name of Christ about her life as a captive in a communist country. She and her son, then 12 years old, escaped while in Vienna and eventually came to America—the country she loved so dearly. Dr. Nikol has a testimony that will blow you away and her love for Christ shines through every word she says. Anyway, she and her sweet piano accompanist, Amy Bogner came and played all of John's favorite hymns and Margaret, at the request of our children and grandchildren, gave us her testimony. That afternoon was a day none of us will ever forget. John was overjoyed that she would do this for him while he was still alive to enjoy it. Oftentimes I think about that day, all of us in the sunroom listening to the love of God poured out in song and the beautiful music of a violin and piano, truly a blessing that continues to ring in my heart.

LOOK AT THE WORD REST. *Matthew 11:29-30–"Take My yoke upon you and learn from Me, for I am gentle and lowly in heart, and you will find rest for your souls. "For My yoke is easy and My burden is light."*

OBSERVE HOW JESUS USED IT IN THIS VERSE.

VERIFY USING OTHER SCRIPTURES.

EXPLAIN A TIME WHEN YOU OR SOMEONE YOU LOVE
NEEDED OR NOW NEEDS THIS KIND OF REST.

Father, thank You that we can and do find rest—true rest-in Jesus. He has no rules, no expectations, no qualifications that He puts on us other than that we believe in Him for our eternal life. There were times when John and I both felt like we still had one more thing to do; one more doctor to see; one more clinical trial to try. But in reality, You spoke through Jack that day and reminded John that the fight was done. I still remember the look of relief that swept over John's face that afternoon and because of the joy You had placed in his heart, he never questioned whether or not he was doing the right thing. Thank you, Lord.

A LIFETIME OF LOVE

June 26, 2013, 6:07 p.m.

How on earth will we pack into two weeks a lifetime of love, remembering and faith? In our own strength, we can't... BUT GOD! Praying, remembering, loving, listening, enjoying, savoring every second of the days and every snore of the nights! The sun is warmer, the stars are brighter and the heavens are declaring the glory of God.

None of this negates the fact that our hearts are breaking for US—not for him, however. He will soon leave this world and all its troubles and instead live REAL LIFE in the home that Jesus has prepared for him. Oh how I long to be able to go there with him, but unless God intervenes, I shall wait until the day that God has chosen to be my last here on this side of eternity.

Please pray for God's mercy for John and His peace and comfort for us, his family and know that we pray for you, our friends who have traveled this journey with us thus far and supported us in prayer. We love you all, Dian

Lest you think any of this was easy and that I just kept my eyes on Jesus and didn't ever get upset, let me assure you that didn't happen. On July 4, when all of the children and their children and my sisters Paula and Kay and John's sister, Karen, were there, my insides were shaking and I felt like I would explode! I turned to the ones in the bedroom with us and said, "I've got to get out of here. I think I'm gonna explode!" They all looked at me with huge eyes as I ran out of that room. I hit the door to the patio and screamed so loud I think my parents in heaven heard it. I screamed and ran and screamed some more! I pleaded with God to STOP THIS SUFFERING! HOW MUCH LONGER IS THIS GOING TO LAST! WHY, OH WHY, WON'T DEATH COME? TEACH ME THE LESSON SO HE CAN GO HOME! Our daughter Courtney just held me and let me scream. People were walking up and down the street staring. I screamed until I could scream no more. But not before asking God if He even heard me. I felt as if He had abandoned me as He ministered to John. After all, I reasoned that surely John was taking all of His time! Just at that moment, of all things, a dove flew into the bushes right next to where Courtney and I were sitting. He seemed wounded. Courtney's husband Greg, and my sister Paula came around to the front yard and we showed them the dove. I remember one of them picking him up, and when I looked at him, it was as if I heard God say—"I am here and I understand. Be still and know that I AM GOD." He then flew off. God has the most wonderful ways of letting us know exactly what we need to know. I thought of Psalm 55:2-6 where David was crying out the Lord: *"Attend to me, and hear me; I am restless in my complaint, and moan noisily, Because of the voice of the enemy, Because of the oppression of the wicked; For they bring down trouble upon me, And in wrath they hate me. My heart is severely pained within me, And the terrors of death have fallen upon me. Fearfulness and trembling have come upon me, And horror has overwhelmed me. So I said, "Oh, that I had wings like a dove! I would fly away and be at rest."* I only wanted John to fly away to Jesus and be at rest.

My Father, how I thank You that only a few days later
my John did fly to Jesus and was, at last, at rest.

The last Sunday of his life, our dear friends Jan Johnson, Scott McEwen and Dave Anderson brought communion elements so that we could all have communion together. Both of my sisters, Paula and Kay; John's sister Karen; our dear friends Gwen and Hack and our children and several grandchildren were there. John was in and out of consciousness at that point, but it was a special time. That night I crawled into the hospital bed with John and whispered to him that I would follow through with every single thing he had asked of me. I told him that I was sorry for every word I ever said that had hurt him, but that I hoped he knew that he was the love of my life. He squeezed my hand and a tear ran down his cheek. My tears covered his face as I prayed over him. I felt the presence of Jesus in that room as 10,000 Reasons played on the CD player.

One of my favorite accounts of John's journey was the night we all thought he would die. He was barely breathing and he looked awful and struggled to even get comfortable. All of us were around his bed and Scott leaned in and said, "Dad, remember when we used to go fishing early in the morning before the sun was even up? Remember how excited we always were? Just imagine if very early in the morning the greatest Fisher of Men the world has ever known comes to take you with Him." Erin, Courtney and I stood around the bed crying. At four o'clock that next morning, John began to get excited. I called everyone to come downstairs. But it wasn't God's timing to take him that day. However, I wonder if John got a glimpse of that Great Fisher of Men.

On July 10, 2013, at 10:45 p.m. while I was holding his hand and he was close to going home, I said to him, "Baby, when you see Jesus, He will take your breath away!" It wasn't two seconds later that he opened his eyes, and went, "HAAAH!" He had seen his Savior.

Right there in our bedroom, he saw Jesus! Everyone came running into our bedroom so that we could all talk to him for we knew he could hear us. We held him and spoke and sang for quite a while. It was a special time for all of us knowing that he was absent from the body, at home with the Lord!

The morning after he passed into glory, our grandson, Jon Wiley and granddaughter, Hope, came into the bedroom to say good morning to Abba as they had been doing since he'd been on Hospice. They would hold his hand and talk to him, and then they'd go in the kitchen and have breakfast. When they came in that morning his bed was empty, so they ran into the bathroom where I was putting on my face and said, "Nanny, where is Abba?" I took them by the hands and said, "Last night Jesus came and took Abba to his home in Heaven!" They said, "YAY FOR ABBA! YAY FOR JESUS!" Then they ran into the kitchen. I followed them in there, and little Devyn, who had been with us the night before as Abba breathed his last said, "I already knew that because I was there!" They were quiet for a minute, then Jon said, "Well! I didn't know we could stay up and WATCH!" I love the innocence of children! How precious was this?

I walked in pure joy for the first three days after Jesus took John home. I was more than happy for him. He and I had talked for eight years about what it must be like to see Jesus face to face. I KNOW THAT he saw Jesus face that night as he took his last breath on earth and his first breath in heaven. Our children were with me until the Sunday after his service, and all of us remembered and laughed and cried together. Then they all went home...then they all went home... Then. They. All. Went. Home. That night when I went into our bedroom, I cried out to God—PLEASE TAKE THAT VISION OF JOHN LYING IN THAT HOSPITAL BED OUT OF MY MIND! I got into the shower crying out to God about that. I clearly heard a gentle voice say to me, "Dian, I took him home in this bedroom—this is Holy Ground." I never saw that sight again.

Since that night I have cried buckets of tears and felt like my heart had been ripped out of my chest. I had never not been married. I didn't know how to live as a single woman. I kinda just went through the motions of living. I went to BSF on Tuesdays and Wednesdays, I went to church on Sundays. I kind of settled into a routine of "doing," but I tried not to feel. Mother Teresa once said, "The most terrible problem in the world today is loneliness." I, for the first time ever, understood what she meant. Larry Crabb describes hell as "being alone forever." THAT I can't imagine. I knew Jesus was with me, but I longed to have John put his strong arms around me just one more time. I missed everything about him—the smell of his cologne, his voice, how he always knew what I needed before I did, his wise counsel when I would be upset with people. On November 11, I said to Him, "God, I just want him for one more minute. Please, please, please hear my prayer. Just one more minute." Dave and Betty had come over just a few days or so before, and I had asked Dave to talk to me again about the OKIE DOKIE—my way of remembering the oiketerion, which is a Greek word for the garment that God gives His children to wear that covers the pallor of death and clothes them until we get our resurrected bodies and beautiful white robes. It's mentioned in the book of Jude and 2 Corinthians 5:2, which is my favorite as it reads, "For in this we groan, earnestly desiring to be clothed with our habitation which is from heaven, if indeed, having been clothed, we shall not be found naked." I walked in the backyard praying and crying when suddenly, I smelled the fragrance that John always wore! I stopped and said, "ARE YOU HERE?" I heard the word oiketerion in my head and looked up, and right above me was a beautiful cloud that had rainbows swirling around in it. It took my breath away. I fell to my knees crying and thanking God that He had heard my plea, and He alone knew that those two things were so very important to me. I had perfect peace that passes all understanding from that moment on and joy filled my heart! I felt like I could live again. I remembered that John had said to me he wanted me to **embrace life** and not grieve forever.

LOOK AT 2 COR. 5:2-4. *For we know that if our earthly house, this tent, is destroyed, we have a building from God, a house not made with hands, eternal in the heavens. For in this we groan, earnestly desiring to be clothed with our habitation which is from heaven, if indeed, having been clothed, we shall not be found naked. For we who are in this tent groan, being burdened, not because we want to be unclothed, but further clothed, that mortality may be swallowed up by life.*

OBSERVE carefully the words tent, house, habitation, clothed.

VERIFY how temporary they are.

EXPLAIN your feelings about being clothed in something not made with hands but by GOD!

Father God, You are the only One who would have known what was important to me that day. You knew I needed to feel Your Presence and John's closeness, and You knew that his fragrance was so important to me. And You knew that the okieterioin was something I had been so blessed to hear about. Thank you that You are such a personal God— living in me by the Power of the Holy Spirit.

NO OTHER GODS

Our son Scott painted a very life-like portrait of John and gave it to me for Christmas. It is about 3' X 5' and looks just like him. After I hung it in the living room, I would walk by and talk to him. Each night when I would really be lonely, I would stand there and tell him how much I missed him. I would ask him to help me get through this terrible loss. In fact, I talked to him all the time. On one particular day, I was having my quiet time and asking the Lord why I felt so stuck in my grief, after all, He had been so gracious as to give me that sweet experience in the backyard in November and had given me joy and peace. What was going on now? In my heart I heard, "THOU SHALL HAVE NO OTHER GODS BEFORE ME." What? "THOU SHALL HAVE NO OTHER GODS BEFORE ME!" I said, "Lord, I have no idols..." Then it struck me! I had been talking to a PAINTING rather than praying to GOD! Only a few weeks before that I had counseled a lady who told me she prayed to Mary and never got an answer to her prayers and I told her, "Well, of course not! Mary is dead! You need to pray to God! He hears your prayers, not Mary!" Here I was doing the same thing. I got on my knees and asked for forgiveness immediately, and do you know what? The gates of heaven swung open and my joy and my peace returned! I was back in fellowship with the One who made me, redeemed me, saved me, is sanctifying me and will glorify me when at last I see Him face to face! NO GREATER JOY—MAXIMUM JOY!

THE BEST IS YET TO COME

Every upset in your life—EVERY SINGLE ONE—is a chance for an encounter with our glorious God. I don't yet know what He has in mind for me for the rest of my life, but I know His Word says He is my husband, and wow, just imagine having a perfect husband! But, I plan to keep my eyes on the prize because, THE BEST IS YET TO COME! GOD WINS AND MAKES ALL THINGS NEW!

Each day was another step toward a new normal for me. One day I was asking God, "How long will it be before I stop grieving and longing for John?" That very afternoon I got a note from a friend of Courtney's which read—

"The reality is you will grieve forever. You will NOT "get over" the loss of a loved one. You WILL learn to live with it. You will heal and you will rebuild yourself around the loss you have suffered. You will be whole again but you will never be the same again. Nor should you want to." Elizabeth Kugler-Ross

That is exactly what I needed to know, and it is one of the truest statements I have ever read. "I will never be the same again, but I wouldn't want to be." Why? Because it's changed me in so many ways. I have learned to do many things because I've had to learn them, things I never knew I could do. I've learned I am stronger than I thought I was. Smarter than I thought I was. Able to do things I never thought I would do without someone like John showing me teaching me how to do them. I am a softer version of my old self. More patient. More kind. Not as structured. More accepting, more loving, more laidback. Not in such a hurry over nothing! (Well, perhaps my driving hasn't changed all that much.) I have learned what's really important on this earth. The only two things that are forever are people and the Word of God. I learned that I was to invest in those two things because that's what would count for the Kingdom—people and God's Word.

On December 7, 2015, I was at Bible Study Fellowship and I was both humbled and blown away to be able to share something that I only realized God had done for me the Wednesday before. We were studying Revelation 6 and there was a question that read, *"What does Psalm 46 tell us about God that gives substantial help during difficult times, and where do you take refuge for today's trials and the coming judgments?"* I turned in my bible to Psalm 46 and began to read it, but before I could finish I noticed a note I had written in my bible on July 10, 2008. "God is our refuge and strength, a very present help in trouble." The note said at verse 1, "John fell in the bathroom." On the opposite margin I had written, "July 10, 2013—my John just saw Jesus face to face." The scripture I had underlined was also from Psalm 46, but it was from verse 10: "Be still and know that I AM God." Then I saw what God had done. He had been with me on July 10, 2008, when I called out to Him for help, and five years to the day later, He had been with me as John breathed his last breath on earth and his first breath in heaven. Immanuel—God with us. With me. With John. With our family and our friends. With all who call out to Him—He is Immanuel, God with us.

It was a day or so later that I realized that not only was John right in saying that joy had descended on him that day back in February of 2013, but it had also descended on me in 2015. Gradually, I had begun to actually feel what John had felt. A joy that was tangible and inexplicable—a joy that had bubbled up from within and covered me on the outside! It was, as Peter said in *1 Peter 1:8,9*—*"…whom having not seen you love. Though now you do no see Him, yet believing, you rejoice with joy inexpressible and full of glory, receiving the end of your faith—the salvation of your souls."*

Joy. For all those years, we walked in joy because that's what God had told us to do. Those verses He gave us at the beginning that were all about joy were transforming, not only for us as we remembered them in the hard times and in the good, but also for others who were watching. A little three letter word that our whole family learned could and would change our lives every single day that we chose to obey. Soon after Jesus took John home I realized—joy isn't just a word, it isn't just a lifestyle—it's Jesus. It's Jesus. Jesus already lived in me by the power of the Holy Spirit, but since I had chosen to obey Him by choosing joy in this journey, I realized He was not only with me but WITH ME! All over me! Everywhere and all the time—Jesus. He had descended on me and there was no going back to a lack of understanding—no going back to thinking I was alone or afraid or unable to function. I realized that Joy and Jesus are one in the same. There is no joy apart from Jesus—there can be happiness, but that depends on circumstances. Joy comes from a place deep within, and it comes from knowing that no matter what happens on this earth, this is not all there is. It comes from knowing that because I am IN CHRIST, my future is secure. Just like John—JOY descended upon me, and I can hardly wait to get to the other side and see the face of JOY, my Jesus—and of course, my John.

THE OTHER SIDE
Martha Snell Nicholson

This isn't death—it's glory, this isn't dark—it's light;
It isn't stumbling, groping, or even faith—it's sight!
This isn't grief or having my last tear wiped away,
It's sunrise and it's morning of my eternal day.

It isn't even praying—it's speaking face to face,
It's listening and glimpsing the wonders of His grace;
For this is the end of pleading for strength to bear my pain,
Not even pain's dark memory will ever live again.

How did I bear this earth life before I came up higher?
Before my soul was granted its every deep desire;
Before I knew this rapture of meeting face to face
The One who sought me, saved me, and kept me by His grace!

www.ingramcontent.com/pod-product-compliance
Lightning Source LLC
LaVergne TN
LVHW051606080426
835510LV00020B/3158